# Parables of the Cross

## by

## I. Lilias Trotter.

Marshall Brothers, Ltd.
London & Edinburgh.

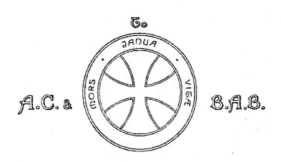

To

A.C. &      B.A.B.

JANUA · VIGÆ · MORS

in memory of lessons
learnt together

# Parables of the Cross

I. Lilias Trotter

## Death is the Gate of Life

There was deep insight in those old words. For man's natural thought of death is that of a dreary ending in decay and dissolution. And from his standpoint he is right: death as the punishment of sin *is* an ending.

But far other is God's thought in the redemption of the world. He takes the very thing that came in with the curse, and makes it the path of glory. Death becomes a beginning instead of an ending, for it becomes the means of liberating a fresh life.

And so the hope that lies in these parable lessons of death and life is meant for those only who are turning to Him for redemption. To those who have *not* turned, death stands in all its old awful doom, inevitable, irrevocable. There is no gleam of light through it for them.

\* \* \* \* \* \* \* \*

"The death of the Cross"—death's triumph hour—that was the point where God's gate opened; and to that gate we come again and again, as our lives unfold, and through it pass even on earth to our joyful resurrection, to a life each time more abundant, for each time the dying is a deeper dying. The Christian life is a process of deliverance out of one world into another, and "death," as has been truly said, "is the only way out of any world in which we are."

"Death is the gate of life." Does it look so to us? Have we learnt to go down, once and again, into its gathering shadows in quietness and confidence, knowing that there is always "a better resurrection" beyond?

It is in the stages of a plant's growth, its budding and blossoming and seed-bearing, that this lesson has come to me: the lesson of death in its delivering power. It has come as no mere far-fetched imagery, but as one of the many voices in which God speaks, bringing strength and gladness from His Holy Place.

Can we not trace the sign of the Cross in the first hint of the new spring's dawning? In many cases, as in the chestnut, before a single old leaf has faded, next year's buds may be seen, at the summit of branch and twig, formed into its very likeness: in others the leaf-buds seem to bear its mark by breaking through the stem blood-red. Back in the plant's first stages, the crimson touch is to be found in seed-leaves and fresh shoots, and even in the hidden sprouts. Look at the acorn, for instance, as it breaks its shell, and see how the baby tree bears its birthmark: it is the blood-red in which the prism ray dawns out of the darkness, and the sunrise out of the night. The very stars, science now tells us, glow with this same colour as they are born into the universe out of the dying of former stars.[1]

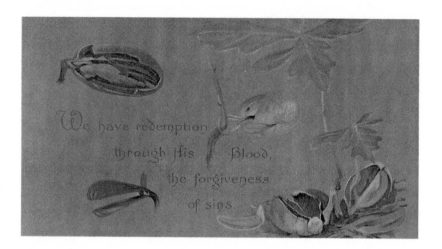

Be it as it may in nature, it is true, at any rate in the world of grace, that each soul that would enter into real life must bear at the outset this crimson seal; there must be the individual "sprinkling of the Blood of Jesus Christ." It must go out through the Gate of the Cross.

And here is the needs-be. Death is the only way out of the world of condemnation wherein we lie. Shut into that world, it is vain to try by any self-effort to battle out; nothing can revoke the decree "the soul that sinneth it shall die."

The only choice left is this. Shall it be, under the old headship of Adam, our own death, in all that God means by the word, or shall it be, under the headship of Christ, the death of another in our place?

It is when we come to self-despair, when we feel ourselves locked in, waiting our doom, that the glory and the beauty of God's way of escape dawns upon us, and we submit ourselves to Him in it. All resistance breaks down as faith closes on the fact: "He loved me and gave Himself for me." We receive the atonement so hardly won, and we go out into life not only pardoned, but cleared and justified.

## Death to Sin's Penalty is the Way Out into a Life of Justification.

And as we go out free, we find that on the other side of the Cross a new existence has really begun: that the love of the Crucified has touched the springs of our being—we are in another world, under an open heaven. "Christ hath suffered for sins, the Just for the unjust, that He might bring us to God."

Does anyone read these words who is trying to struggle from the natural life into the spiritual, by "some other way" than this way of the Cross? It is as impossible as it would be to pass from to-day into to-morrow except through the night. Your battling is a battling against God. Yield and come to His terms. Yield now.

\* \* \* \* \* \* \* \*

But blessed as it is, this passage into a life of peace with Him, woe to the soul that stops there, thinking that the goal is reached, and dwindles, so to speak, into a stunted bud. Holiness, not safety, is the end of our calling.

And so it comes to pass that a fresh need for deliverance is soon pressed upon him who is true to God's voice in his heart. The two lives are there together, one new-born and feeble, the other strong with an earlier growth. "The flesh lusteth against the spirit and the spirit against the flesh," and the will power is distracted between the two, like the sap that flows partly into the old condemned leaves, partly into the fresh buds. Consequently there is the strife of a kingdom divided against itself: sometimes the one life grows and flourishes, sometimes the other; sometimes they struggle on side by side, till the cry is forced out—"Oh, wretched man that I am; who shall deliver me?"

And here again, when the point of self-despair is reached, and we come to see that our efforts after holiness are as vain as our efforts after acceptance with God, the door of escape opens afresh.

For there *is* glory be to God, a definite way out from the prison life of sruggling and failure, sinning and repenting, wherein many a soul beats its wings for years after the question of pardon has been settled. And that way is again the way of death.

A stage of dying must come over the plant before the new leaves can grow and thrive. There must be a deliberate choice between the former growth and the new; one must give way to the other; the acorn has to come to the point where it ceases to keep its rag of former existence, and lets everything go to the fresh shoot: the twig must withdraw its sap from last year's leaf, and let it flow into this year's bud.

And before the soul can really enter upon a life of holiness, with all its blessed endless possibilities, a like choice must be made: all known sin must be deliberately given up, that the rising current may have its full play.

"But," you say, "I have tried again and again to give up sin: I have prayed, and I have resolved, but the will finds its way back into the old channels, and is keeping alive the past before I know it."

Look at our parable. If you picked off one of the dead leaves and examined the leaf-stalk through a microscope, you would find that the old channel is silted up by a barrier invisible to the naked eye. The plant has shut the door on the last year's leaf, condemning it to decay, and soon without further effort the stalk loosens, the winds of God play around it, and it falls away.

But where is the barrier that we can place between ourselves and the old nature? Where is the sentence of death that we can pass upon it?

Back to the Cross again! It is there, within our reach. "Our old man is crucified with Him, that the body of sin might be destroyed, that henceforth we should not serve sin; for he that is dead is freed from sin."

Death to Sin is the Way Out into a Life of Holiness.

The Cross of our Lord Jesus Christ shuts off the life of sin; like the silted-up channel, it stands a blessed invisible barrier between us and sinning, as we "reckon" it there: that is, hold it there by faith and will. And His open grave is the open way into a life, wherein our rising powers can develop into all their spring vigour.

The sap—the will—the "ego"—is withdrawn from the former existence, its aims and desires, and is sent into the new. It is given over to the other side: we hold to it that *this* is now our life, the only one that has the right to be. We reckon ourselves dead to the old; we reckon ourselves alive to the new; "putting off" the former, "putting on" the latter.

Take a practical instance. An old habit of doubting and fearing asserts itself in your soul, alive and strong. You have two things to do. Close the door upon the doubt: shut your eyes to it: reckon yourself dead to it.

And then reckon into life the new-born growth of faith in your soul, and put all your force into believing: lift up your eyes to the God in Whom you believe: believe in the teeth of everything, as if the cause for doubt were not there. Then the sap, ceasing from feeding the old shoot, will flow into the new.

But is it an act, or a gradual process, this "putting off the old man?" It is both. It is a resolve taken once for all, but carried out in detail day by day. The first hour that the sap begins to withdraw, and the leaf-stalk begins to silt up, the leaf's fate is sealed: there is never a moment's reversal of the decision. Each day that follows is a steady carrying out of the plant's purpose: "this old leaf shall die, and the new leaf shall live." So with your soul. Come to the decision once for all: "every known sin shall go—if there is a deliverance to be had, I will have it." Put the Cross of Christ, in its mysterious delivering power, *irrevocably* between you and sinning, and hold on there. That is your part, and you must do it. There is no further progress possible to you, till you make up your mind to part company with every sin in which you know you are indulging—every sin of thought, word, or deed, every link with the world, the flesh, or the devil, everything on which the shadow of a question falls, as God's light shines in: to part company, not by a series of gradual struggles, but by an honest act of renouncing, maintained by faith and obedience. And as you make the decision up to your present knowledge, you must determine that this is henceforth your attitude towards *all* that is "not of the Father," as His growing light shall reveal it.

From His side God will come in with a breath of His resurrection power; for the Cross and the empty tomb cannot be long divided. The law of the Spirit of Life can work now, as you deliberately loose hold of all clinging to sin; the expulsive power of His working within, and the play of His winds around, will make you "free indeed," like these young shoots when last year's leaves have fallen.

\* \* \* \* \* \* \* \*

This brings us to the positive side; for when the sentence of death on the old nature is realised, the new nature can be manifested. Separation from all known sin is the starting-point for santification, not the goal: it is only the negative side of holiness; it is only reaching the place where God can develop His ideal in us unhindered. It is when the death of winter has done its work that the sun can draw out in each plant its own individuality, and make its existence full and fragrant. Holiness means something more than the sweeping away of the old leaves of sin: it means the life of Jesus developed in us.

The law of the Spirit of Life.

No matter if we feel utterly helpless before that lovely life of His. Given the conditions—the hidden power within, and the old outlets of growth shut off—the sun will do the rest; out of the midst of apparent lifelessness, of barrenness, of difficulty, the blossoms will be drawn forth. Do not let us "limit the Holy One of Israel" by putting off His power to work this miracle into a distant future. How hopeless the naked wood of a fruit tree would look to us in February if we had never seen the marvel of springtime! Yet the heavenly bloom bursts straight out, with hardly an intermediate step of new growth.

Look again at a flowering rush. The crest breaks forth from nothingness—out of the lifeless-seeming pith come crowding the golden brown blossoms, till there is hardly "room to receive" them. What more do we need for our souls than to have this God for our God?

Brought forth by the Sun.

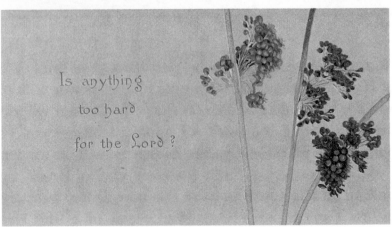

Is anything too hard for the Lord?

Once allow the manifestation of His grace in these poor hearts of ours to be a miracle, and there is no need to defer it vaguely. How many of the wonders wrought by Christ on earth lay in concentrating the long processes of nature into a sudden act of power. The sick would, many of them, have been healed by degrees in the ordinary course of things; the lapse of years would have brought about the withering of the fig-tree; the storm would have spent itself in few hours. The miracle in each case consisted in the slow process being quickened by the Divine breath, and condensed into a moment.

Cannot we trust Him for like marvels in our souls? There, too, "a day is with the Lord as a thousand years." There is no needs be on His part that He should prolong this first act of makings us holy over the rest of our lives. A miracle—a wonder—is all that we need, and "He is the God, that doeth wonders." Satan is quite content that we should have faith for future sanctification, just as he was content that we should have faith for future salvation. It is when the soul rises to *"here and now"* that he trembles.

Whatever is the next grace for your soul, can you believe for its supply at once, straight out from the dry, bare need? Christ's process is very simple and very swift: "Whatsoever things ye desire, when ye pray, believe that ye receive them, and ye shall have them."

And not only with the barrenness of our souls can God deal with His quickening breath, but with our difficulties as well: with those things in our surroundings that seem the most unfavourable.

See this bit of gorse-bush. The whole year round the thorn has been hardening and sharpening. Spring comes: the thorn does not drop off, and it does not soften; there it is, as uncompromising as ever; but half-way up appear two brown furry balls, mere specks at first, that break at last—straight out of last year's thorn—into a blaze of fragrant golden glory.

See this bit of gorse-bush. The whole year round the thorn has been hardening and sharpening. Spring comes: the thorn does not drop off, and it does not soften; there it is, as uncompromising as ever; but half-way up appear two brown furry balls, mere specks at first, that break at last—straight out of last year's thorn—into a blaze of fragrant golden glory.

"Now no chastening for the present seemeth to be joyous, but grievous; nevertheless afterward it yieldeth the peaceable fruit of righteousness unto them that are exercised thereby." Never mind if the trouble shews no sign of giving way: it is just when it seems most hopelessly unyielding, holding on through the spring days, alive and strong, it is *then* that the tiny buds appear that soon will clothe it with glory. Take the very hardest thing in your life—*the* place of difficulty, outward or inward, and expect God to triumph gloriously in that very spot. Just there He can bring your soul into blossom!

* * * * * * * *

And so the spring-time expands, till it passes once more into the shadow of Calvary. For the blessedness of receiving is not all that God has for us: a new world lies beyond—a world of giving: a giving first to God in surrender, then to man in sacrifice.

A flower that stops short at its flowering misses its purpose. We were created for more than our own spiritual development; reproduction, not mere development, is the goal of matured being—reproduction in other lives. There is a tendency in some characters, running parallel to the high cultivation that spends its whole energy on the production of bloom at the expense of seed. The flowers that are bent on perfecting themselves, by becoming double, end in barrenness, and a like barrenness comes to the soul whose interests are all concentrated upon its own spiritual well-being, heedless of the needs around. The true, ideal flower is the one that uses its gifts as means to an end; the brightness and sweetness are not for its own glory; they are but to attract the bees and butterflies that will fertilise and make it fruitful. All may go when the work is done—"it is more blessed to give than to receive."

And we ourselves are "saved to save"—we are made to give—to let everything go if only we may have more to give. The pebble takes in all the rays of light that fall on it, but the diamond flashes them out again: every little facet is a means, not simply of drinking more in, but of giving more out. The unearthly loveliness of the opal arises from the same process, carried on *within* the stone: the microscope shows it to be shattered through and through with numberless fissures that catch and refract and radiate every ray that they can seize.

Yes, there lies before us a beautiful *possible* life—one that shall have a passion for giving: that shall be poured forth to God—spent out for man: that shall be consecrated "for the hardest work and the darkest sinners." But how are we to enter in? How are we to escape from the self-life that holds us, even after the sin-life has loosed its grasp?

Back to the Cross: not only from the world of condemnation and from the world of sinning does it free us as we accept it, but from the power of outward things and from the thraldom of self: not only does it open the door into the world of acquittal, and again into that of holiness, but yet again into the new realm of surrender, and thence into that of sacrifice. For the essential idea of the Cross is a life lost to be found again in those around.

Let us look at God's picturing. As the plant develops there comes a fresh stage of yielding. At first it was only the dead, disfiguring leaves that had to go—now it is the fair new petals: they must fall, and for no visible reason—no one seems enriched by the stripping.

And the first step into the realm of giving is a like surrender—not manward, but Godward: an utter yielding of our best. So long as our idea of surrender is limited to the renouncing of unlawful things, we have never grasped its true meaning: *that* is not worthy of the name for "no polluted thing" can be offered.

The life lost on the Cross was not a sinful one—the treasure poured forth there was God-given, God-blessed treasure, lawful and right to be kept: only that there was the life of the world at stake!

Death to Lawful Things is the Way Out into a Life of Surrender.

Look at this buttercup as it begins to learn its new lesson. The little hands of the calyx clasp tightly in the bud, round the beautiful petals; in the young flower their grasp grows more elastic—loosening somewhat in the daytime, but keeping the power of contracting, able to close in again during a rainstorm, or when night comes on. But see the central flower, which has reached its maturity. The calyx hands have unclasped utterly now— they have folded themselves back, past all power of closing again upon the petals, leaving the golden crown free to float away when God's time comes.

Have we learned the buttercup's lesson yet? Are our hands off the very blossom of our life? Are all things— even the treasures that He has sanctified—held loosely, ready to be parted with, without a struggle, when He asks for them?

It is not in the partial relaxing of grasp, with power to take back again, that this fresh victory of death is won: it is won when that very power of taking back is yielded; when our hands, like the little calyx hands of God's buttercups, are not only taken off, but folded behind our back in utter abandonment. Death means a loosened grasp—loosened beyond all power of grasping again.

And it is no strange thing that happens to us, if God takes us at our word, and strips us for a while of all that made life beautiful. It may be outward things—bodily comfort, leisure, culture, reputation, friendships—that have to drift away as our hands refuse to clasp on anything but God's will for us. Or it may be on our inner life that the stripping falls, and we have to leave the sunny lands of spiritual enjoyment for one after another of temptation's battlefields, where every inch of our foothold has to be tested, where even, it may seem to give way—till no experience, no resting-place remains to us in heaven or earth but God Himself—till we are "wrecked upon God."

Have faith, like the flowers, to let the old things go. Earn His beatitude, His "Blessed is he, whosoever shall not be offended in Me"—"the beatitude of the trusting," as it has well been called—even if you have to earn it like John the Baptist in an hour of desolation. You have told Him that you want Him only. Are you ready to ratify the words when His emptying begins to come? Is God enough? Is it still "*My* God" that you cry, even as Jesus cried when nothing else was left Him?

Yes, practical death with Him to lawful things is just *letting* go, even as He on the Cross let go all but God. It is not to be reached by struggling for it, but simply by yielding as the body yields at last to the physical death that lays hold on it—as the dying calyx yields its flower. Only to no iron law with its merciless grasp do we let ourselves go, but into the hands of the Father: it is there that our spirit falls, as we are made conformable unto the death of Jesus.

Does all this seem hard? Does any soul, young in this life and in that to come, shrink back and say "I would rather keep in the springtime—I do not want to reach unto the things that are before if it must mean all this of pain."

To such comes the Master's voice: "Fear none of those things which thou shalt suffer": You are right to be glad in His April days while he gives them. Every stage of the heavenly growth in us is lovely to Him; He is the God of the daisies and the lambs and the merry child hearts! It *may* be that no such path of loss lies before you; there are people like the lands where spring and summer weave the year between them, and the autumn processes are hardly noticed as they come and go. The one thing is to keep obedient in spirit, then you will be ready to let the flower-time pass if He bids you, when the sun of His love has worked some more ripening. You will feel by then that to try to keep the withering blossoms would be to cramp and ruin your soul. It is loss to keep when God says 'give'.

For here again death is the gate of life: it is an entering in, not a going forth only; it means a liberating of new powers as the former treasures float away like the dying petals.

We cannot feel a consciousness of death: the words are a contradiction in terms. If we had literally passed out of this world into the next we should not feel dead, we should only be conscious of a new wonderful life beating within us. Our consciousness of death would be an entirely negative matter—the old pains would be unable to touch us, the old bonds would be unable to fetter us. Our actual consciousness would have passed into the new existence: we should be independent of the old.

And a like independence is the characteristic of the new flood of resurrection life that comes to our souls as we learn this fresh lesson of dying—a grand independence of any earthly thing to satisfy our soul, the liberty of those who have nothing to lose, because they have nothing to keep. We can do without *anything* while we have God. Hallelujah!

Nor is this all. Look at the expression of abandonment about this wild-rose calyx as time goes on, and it begins to grow towards the end for which it has had to count all things but loss: the look of dumb emptiness has gone—it is flung back joyously now, for simultaneously with the new dying a richer life has begun to work at its heart—so much death, so much life—for

> "Ever with death it weaveth
> The warp and woof of the world."

The lovely wild-rose petals that have drifted away are almost forgotten in the "reaching forth unto the things that are before:" the seed-vessel has begun to form: it is "yielded . . . to bring forth fruit."

Yes, there is another stage to be developed in us after the lesson of absolute unquestioning surrender to God has been learnt. A life that has been poured forth to Him must find its crown, its completion, in being poured forth for man: it must grow out of surrender into sacrifice. "They first gave their own selves to the Lord, and unto us by the will of God."

Behind my back I fling,
Like an unvalued thing,
My former self
and ways,
And reaching
forward far
I seek the things that are
Beyond time's
lagging
days.

Back to the Cross once more: if there is any place where this fresh lesson can be learnt, it is there! "Hereby perceive we the love of God, because He laid down His life for us, and we ought to lay down our lives for the brethren." It is the very love of Calvary that must come down into our souls, "Yea, if I be poured forth upon the service of your faith I joy and rejoice with you all:" so spoke the apostle who drank most deeply into the Master's spirit: and again—"Death worketh in us, but life in you." "Neither count I my life dear unto myself, that I may finish . . . the ministry."

Deeper and deeper must be the dying, for wider and fuller is the lifetide that it is to liberate—no longer limited by the narrow range of our own being, but with endless powers of multiplying in other souls. Death must reach the very springs of our nature to set it free: it is not this thing or that thing that must go now: it is blindly, helplessly, recklessly, our very selves. A dying must come upon *all* that would hinder God's working through us—all interests, all impulses, all energies that are "born of the flesh"—all that is merely human and apart from His Spirit. Only thus can the Life of Jesus, in its intensity of love for sinners, have its way in our souls.

Death to Self is the Way Out into a Life of Sacrifice.

This dandelion has long ago surrendered its golden petals, and has reached its crowning stage of dying—the delicate seed-globe must break up now—it gives and gives till it has nothing left.

What a revolution would come over the world—the world of starving bodies at home—the world of starving souls abroad, if something like this were the standard of giving; if God's people ventured on "making themselves poor" as Jesus did, for the sake of the need around; if the "I"—"me"—"mine" were *practically* delivered up, no longer to be recognised when they clash with those needs.

The hour of this new dying is clearly defined to the dandelion globe: it is marked by detachment. There is no sense of wrenching: it stands ready, holding up its little life, not knowing when or where or how the wind that bloweth where it listeth may carry it away. It holds itself no longer for its own keeping, only as something to be given: a breath does the rest, turning the "readiness to will" into the "performance." (2 Cor. 8. 11.) And to a soul that through "deaths oft" has been brought to this point, even acts that look as if they *must* involve an effort, become something natural, spontaneous, full of a "heavenly involuntariness," so simply are they the outcome of the indwelling love of Christ.

Shall we not ask God to convict us, as to where lies the hindrance to this self-emptying? It is not alone mere selfishness, in its ordinary sense, that prevents it; long after this has been cleansed away by the Precious Blood there may remain, unrecognised, the self-life in more subtle forms. It may co-exist with much that looks like sacrifice; there may be much of usefulness and of outward self-denial, and yet below the surface may remain a clinging to our own judgment, a confidence in our own resources, an unconscious taking of our own way, even in God's service. And these things hold down, hold *in* our souls, and frustrate the Spirit in His working. The latent self-life needs to be brought down into the place of death before His breath can carry us hither and thither as the wind wafts the seeds. Are we ready for this last surrender?

I am God, ready to be offered

Measure thy life by loss
and not by gain,
Not by the wine drunk, but
by the wine poured forth,
For love's strength standeth in
love's sacrifice,
And he who suffers most has most to give.

Do you ask "Does God really mean the emptying to reach so far as this?" Study the inner life of Jesus. "I speak not of Myself" He says. "I can of Mine own self do

22

nothing." "I seek not Mine own will, but the will of Him that sent Me." His human self-life, sinless though it was, was laid down that He might live by the Father, and our self-life, defiled and worthless, shall we not lay it down that we may live by Him?

But how? Again not by struggling and wrestling, but by dying to it in Jesus. "I am crucified with Christ"—I myself in the very essence of my being, I let myself go to that death, and by the mysterious power with which God meets faith, I find that He has made it true: the bonds are loosed and He can have His way with me.

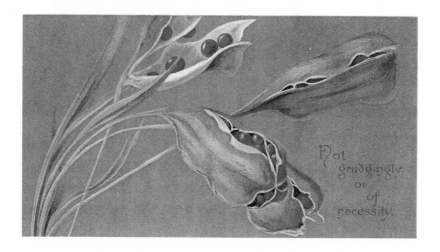

Not grudgingly or of necessity.

See in these wild iris-pods how the last tiny threads must be broken, and with that loosing, all that they have is free for God's use in His world around. All reluctance, all calculating, all *holding in* is gone; the husks are opened wide, the seeds can shed themselves unhindered. Again and again has a breaking come:—the seed broke to let go the shoot—the leaf-bud broke to let go the leaf, and the flower-bud to let go the flower—but all to no practical avail, if there is a holding back now. "Love is the fulfilling of the law," and sacrifice is the very life-breath of love. May God shew us every witholding thread of self that needs breaking still, and may His own touch shrivel it into death.

I will very gladly spend and be spent.

See how this bit of oat-grass is emptying itself out. Look at the wide-openness with which the seed-sheaths loose all that they have to yield, and then the patient content with which they fold their hands—the content of finished work. "She hath done what she could." Oh, the depth of rest that falls on the soul when the voice of the Beloved speaks those words! Will they be said to us?

The seed-vessel hopes for nothing again: it seeks only the chance of shedding itself: its purpose is fulfilled when the wind shakes forth the last seed, and the flower-stalk is beaten low by the autumn storms. It not only spends, but is "spent out" (R. V.) at last. It is through Christ's poverty that we are rich—"as poor" in their turn "yet making many rich" is the mark of those who follow His steps.

Are we following His steps; *are* we? How the dark places of the earth are crying out for all the powers of giving and living and loving that are locked up in hearts at home! How the waste places are pleading dumbly for the treasure that lies there in abundance, stored as it were in the seedvessels of God's garden that have not been broken, not emptied for His world, not freed for His use.

Shall we not free it all gladly.—It is not grudgingly or of necessity that the little caskets break up and scatter the seed, but with the cheerful giving that God loves. Have you ever noticed how often the emptied calyx grows into a diadem, and they stand crowned for their ministry as if they gloried in their power to give as the time draws near?

Even here in measure the faithfulness unto death and the crown of life go together: even here, if we suffer, we shall also reign with Him.

It is when the sun goes out from our horizon to light up the dayspring in far-away lands, that the *glory* of the day comes on: it is in the autumn, when the harvest is gathered and the fruit is stored for the use of man, that the glow of red and gold touches and transfigures bush and tree with a beauty that the summer days never knew.

So with us—The clear pure dawn of cleansing through the Blood—the sunrise gladness of resurrection life; the mid-day light and warmth of growth and service, all are good in their own order: but he who stops short there misses the crown of glory, before which the brightness of former days grows poor and cold. It is when the glow and radiance of a life delivered up to death begins to gather: a life poured forth to Jesus and for His sake to others—it is then that even the commonest things put on a new beauty, as in the sunset, for His life becomes "manifest in our mortal flesh;" a bloom comes on the soul like the bloom on the fruit as its hour of sacrifice arrives.

Oh, that we may learn to die to all that is of self with this royal joyfulness that swallows up death in victory in God's world around! He can make every step of the path full of the triumph of gladness that glows in the golden leaves. Glory be to His Name!

And the outcome, like the outcome of the autumn, is this: there is, a new power set free; a power of multiplying life around. The promise to Christ was that because He poured forth His soul unto death, He should see His seed: and He leads His children in their little measure by the same road. Over and over the promise of seed is linked with sacrifice, as with Abraham and Rebekah and Ruth; those who at His bidding have forsaken all receive an hundred-fold more now in this time, for sacrifice is God's factor in His work of multiplying. "Except a corn of wheat fall into the ground and die, it abideth alone; but if it die, it bringeth forth much fruit."

It is the poured-out life that God blesses—the life that heeds not itself, if only other souls may be won. "Ask and it shall be given unto you" is one of God's nursery lessons to His children. "Give, and it shall be given unto you" comes further on.

The reason is this:—that into the being that is ready to let the self-life go, God the Holy Ghost can come and dwell and work unfettered; and by that indwelling He will manifest within us His wonderful Divine power of *communicating* vitality—of reproducing the image of Jesus in souls around.

It is true that it is a rule that sometimes has exceptions: there are those to whom a blessed life of fruitfulness to God comes in a simple way, with seemingly no hard process of dying involved, just as there are plants that reproduce themselves by bulb and tuber, sucker and shoot, without going through the stripping and scattering that we have been watching. But the law of creation is "the herb yielding seed and the fruit-tree yielding fruit after its kind, whose seed is in itself." And let us count it all joy if this law is carried out in us.

"If it die, it bringeth forth much fruit." Whether it is laid down in toil among the lost, or in travail of soul among His children that Christ be formed in them, either way there will be life brought forth.

It does not follow that every seed will spring up: it is not so in the natural world. The plant's business is to scatter it, not withholding, not knowing which shall prosper, either this or that, or whether they both shall be alike good; once scattered, the responsibility is transferred to the ground that receives it. But the aim of the plant—the goal of all the budding and blossoming and ripening—is that every seed should carry potential life.

Thus are we responsible, not for the tangible results of our ministry to others, but for its being a ministry in demonstration of the Spirit and of power, such a ministry as will make those around us definitely responsible to God for accepting or rejecting the fulness of His salvation. If so, the "signs following" will not be wanting. It will be to the one the savour of death unto death, and to the other the savour of life unto life, but "whether they will hear, or whether they will forbear, they shall know that there hath been a prophet among them."

\* \* \* \* \* \* \* \*

But even when the plant's goal is reached, it is not a finality. "There is no end in nature, but every end is a beginning. Every ultimate fact is only the beginning of a new series."[2] "While the earth remaineth seed-time and harvest . . . shall not cease." Life leads on to new death, and new death back to life again. Over and over when we think we know our lesson, we find ourselves beginning another round of God's Divine spiral: "in deaths oft" is the measure of our growth, *always* delivered unto death for Jesus' sake, that the life also of Jesus might be made manifest in our mortal flesh."

This bit of sphagnum shows the process in miniature: stage after stage of dying has been gone through, and each has been all the while crowned with life. Each time that the crown has sunk down again into death, that death has again been crowned in the act of dying: and the life all the time is the apparent thing: the daily dying that underlies it is out of sight to the passing glance.

Yes, life is the uppermost, resurrection life, radiant and joyful and strong, for we represent down here Him who liveth and was dead and is alive for evermore. Stress had to be laid in these pages on the death gateway, but a gateway is never a dwelling-place; the death-stage is never meant for our souls to stay and brood over, but to pass through with a will into the light beyond. We may and must, like the plants, bear its marks, but they should be visible to God rather than to man, for above all and through all is the inflowing, overflowing life of Jesus: oh let us not dim it by a shadow of morbidness or of gloom: He is not a God of the dead, but a God of the living, and He would have us let the glory of His gladness shine out.

As dying
and
behold
we live.

Think of the wonder of it—the Fountain of Life Himself wells up within us, taking the place of all that we have delivered, bit by bit, into His grave. "I live, yet not I, but Christ liveth in me." Little have we proved, any of us, the resources that lie in that mighty indwelling, little have we learnt what it is to have all our soul-fibres penetrated by its power. May God lead us, no matter what the cost, into all that *can* be known of it, here on earth.

And the results need not end with our earthly days. Should Jesus tarry our works will follow us. The closing in of the signs around us make it seem as if we should not taste of death, and as if the time left us to work and suffer for Him were growing very short; but if that last gate has to be passed before our spirits are sent free into the land of perfect life, God may use, by reason of the wonderful solidarity of His Church, the things that He has wrought in us, for the blessing of souls unknown to us: as these twigs and leaves of bygone years, whose individuality is forgotten, pass on vitality still to the new-born wood-sorrel. God only knows the endless possibilities that lie folded in each one of us!

Shall we not let Him have His way? Shall we not go all lengths with Him in His plans for us—not, as these "green things upon the earth" in their unconsciousness, but with the glory of free choice? Shall we not translate the story of their little lives into our own?

For all their teaching of surrender and sacrifice is no fanciful mysticism; it is a simple reality that can be tested at every turn—nay, that *must* be so tested. If we are apprehending Christ's death in its delivering power, our homes will not be slow to find it out.

\* \* \* \* \* \* \* \*

O Jesus the Crucied I will follow Thee in thy path. Inspire me for the next step, whether it leads down into the shadow of death or up into the light. Surely in what place my Lord the King shall be, whether in death or life, even there also will thy servant be.

Amen.

---

[1] Prof. Huggins. Brit. Asso. 1891.

[2] Emerson

Lightning Source UK Ltd.
Milton Keynes UK
UKOW051402200412

191168UK00001B/292/P